A GIRL'S GUIDE TO BECOMING GREAT:

8 PRINCIPLES FOR A POSITIVE, PROMISING, AND PRODUCTIVE LIFE

A GIRL'S GUIDE TO BECOMING GREAT:

8 PRINCIPLES FOR A POSITIVE, PROMISING, AND PRODUCTIVE LIFE

BY

RHONDA G. MINCEY

3771_3

© 2012 by The RG Mincey Group, LLC. All rights reserved. No part of this publication may be reproduced or transmitted in any form or by any means, electronic or mechanical, including photocopy, recording, or any information storage and retrieval system, without permission in writing from the copyright owner.

ISBN 978-1-61863-393-4

Contact us at:
The RG Mincey Group, LLC.
P. O. Box 1245
Bluffton, SC 29910
www.thergmg.com

The Paradoxical Commandments are reprinted by permission of the author. © Copyright Kent M. Keith 1968, renewed 2001.

All other poems are written by Rhonda G. Mincey, © Copyright 2012. For permission to use them, contact: rhonda@thergmg.com.

The stories are true and some names are changed.

Copy by Rhonda G. Mincey and Darius Anthony
Foreword by Tiffany B. Troutman
Cover Design by Alan Pranke
Edited by Marian Muldrow, Ed. S.

Printed in the United States of America

Table of Contents

About the Young-Adult Writers vii

Preface: A Message to the Girls ix

Preface: A Message to Parents and Facilitators xi

Foreword xiii

Acknowledgements xv

Introduction xvii

Chapter 1: There's More in You 1
Point 1: Don't Limit Yourself 2
Point 2: Average is Not an Option 3
Point 3: You are Full of Potential and Power 4
Affirmation 4
Reflect, Record, Remark, and Respond 5-7
Poem: I Am Made To Be More 8

Chapter 2: You are Uniquely You 9
Point 1: You Become What You Think You Are 10
Point 2: Don't Make Comparisons 12
Point 3: Be Your Own Best Friend 13
Affirmation 13
Reflect, Record, Remark, and Respond 14-16
Poem: I Love Me 17

Chapter 3: Take a Stand 19
Point 1: Maintain Your Values at All Times 19
Point 2: Recognize Your Mistakes and Take a Stand 21
Point 3: Set Your Standards Early 22
Affirmation 23
Reflect, Record, Remark, and Respond 24-27
Poem: Stand Strong 28

Chapter 4: Make Smart Decisions 29
Point 1: Today's Decisions Will Affect Your Future 30
Point 2: Every Decision Has Consequences 32
Point 3: Some Decisions are Life-Changing 33
Affirmation 34
Reflect, Record, Remark, and Respond 35-40
Poem: Choices 41

Chapter 5: Pressures Don't Have to Crush You 43
Point 1: Pressures are Common 43
Point 2: Pressures can be Positive 45
Point 3: You Can Handle Pressures 47
Affirmation 48

Reflect, Record, Remark, and Respond 49-51
Poem: Pressures 52

Chapter 6: Dream It. Do It! 53
Point 1: Go for the Goal... 54
Point 2: What You See is What You'll Become.................................. 56
    4 Steps to Making Your Dream Board 56
Point 3: Dream Big 57
Affirmation 57
Reflect, Record, Remark, and Respond 58-63
Poem: I Dare You 64

Chapter 7: Would You Follow You? 67
Point 1: Lead by Example..67
Point 2: Leaders Follow Other Leaders 69
Point 3: You Can Be a Great Leader 70
Affirmation 71
Reflect, Record, Remark, and Respond 72-75
Poem: The Paradoxical Commandments 76

Chapter 8: The Effects of the Media 77
Point 1: What You Listen to Matters 78
    Music.. 78
Point 2: What You See Matters 79
    Television 79
    Music Videos.. 80
    Advertisements 81
Point 3: What You Say and Show Matters 82
    The Internet and Social Media... 82
Affirmation 84
Reflect, Record, Remark, and Respond 85-88
Poem: The Influence of the Media 89

Resources for Teens and Young Adults 91

Bibliography 97

Notes 99-101

Help Us Help Others 103

Stay Connected 105

About the Author.. 106

ABOUT THE YOUNG-ADULT WRITERS

Darius Anthony is from Claxton, Georgia. He is a graduate of Valdosta State University, in Valdosta, Georgia, where he majored in Criminal Justice. Some of his activities and honors were: Relay for Life Committee, Criminal Justice Academic Achievement Award, Dean's List, Academic Competitiveness Grant, HOPE Scholarship, and Criminal Justice Honor Society (Alpha Phi Sigma). He was also president of Heart of Faith Ministries on Valdosta State University's campus. Darius is currently working on his Master's Degree in Criminal Justice.

Tiffany B. Troutman is a senior at Georgia Institute of Technology in Atlanta, Georgia, majoring in Applied Mathematics. Her career aspiration is to open a preparatory school that focuses on technological global preparation for underprivileged children. She believes that "scholastic achievement is a good thing and that anyone can do math." She is a member of the National Society of Black Engineers and has interned with Proctor and Gamble. She has numerous scholastic achievements and has also served on the board of directors for Leadership for Tomorrow, a nonprofit organization, as well as serving as a peer facilitator for United Way.

PREFACE

A MESSAGE TO THE GIRLS

You hold the power of a positive, promising, and productive life literally in your hands. This book was written especially for you. I chose to write this book to encourage you simply because as a woman, who was once a girl your age, it is my obligation to help you on your journey to be all that God has called you to be. Oftentimes, adults blame you for mistakes you've made, the way you dress, or because you may not "talk" or "act like" a lady. However, with proper support, you can form respectable habits, make wise decisions, and become successful women who leave your mark in your community, and even the world.

I want you to know that regardless of your circumstances or your past, greatness is inside of you. I also want you to make better choices about everyday decisions and for you to reach your full potential. Lastly, always remember that you are beautiful, valuable, and loved. You are a phenomenal young woman and destined for greatness.

Believing in you,

Rhonda G. Mincey

Rhonda G. Mincey
The RG Mincey Group, LLC

PREFACE

A MESSAGE TO PARENTS AND FACILITATORS

Our young girls are losing the struggle every day to "fit-in" and find their place in society; consequently, they are engaging in risky behaviors, such as, dropping out of school, using drugs, and being promiscuous. Many of them are losing hope and have no sense of purpose or direction.

That's why I have devoted nearly a decade of my life to mentoring girls and formed The RG Mincey Group, LLC. Girls everywhere need to know that they matter and greatness is inside of them. During some of my workshops, an astounding number of young girls have told me that they don't believe that they are beautiful. Needless to say, this deeply concerned and saddened me. Here are some real case studies from some of my workshops:

Case 1: While I was conducting a workshop, I noticed that one of the girls in my session had strikingly beautiful eyes, but behind them was what appeared to be sadness. After the session, I complimented her on her eyes, and she looked surprised. I asked her did she think that her eyes were pretty. She replied, "No." I asked her had anyone ever told her that her eyes were pretty and she again said, "No." I thought how sad it was that no one had affirmed her beauty. How even sadder was the fact that she had to hear it from me – a total stranger. I hope that when she now looks in the mirror, she sees a beautiful young woman looking back at her through eyes that are gorgeous and mesmerizing.

Case 2: In a different workshop, a teenage girl said that she doesn't feel that she's beautiful. I asked her what she does when she feels this way. She hesitantly said that sometimes she turns to boys to make her feel pretty.

Case 3: In still another workshop, I asked girls to name five positive adjectives to describe them. Hardly any of them could name three adjectives without struggling and being prompted to do so. Finally, after one of the girls read her adjectives, I asked her was that a difficult task for her to complete. She said, "Yes, because I've never thought about myself like that before."

These are different girls in different situations, but the commonality among them is that they all lack affirmation and are seeking validation. It is our responsibility to tell our girls that they are beautiful, valuable, important, intelligent, witty, "got it goin' on," etc. How often should this be done? Girls should be affirmed every day if possible because they are being bombarded with negative images about their identity; consequently, they are trying to "fit in" as best they can. If we, those people who are closest to them, who love them, and who they look up to, don't positively affirm them, they will seek affirmation from someone else.

I hope that you join me in my mission to change the mindset of our girls. I encourage you to use this book to share the life-changing principles in each chapter with a young lady.

In partnership with you and believing in them, I am phenomenally yours,

Rhonda G. Mincey, Giver of Hope

Rhonda G. Mincey

The RG Mincey Group, LLC

FOREWORD
(From a College Honor Student)

Aspire to Reach Higher

The principles in this book are the principles that I embrace and apply to my life. They have made a huge impact in my life, and I believe that they can do the same for you. I believe that knowing who you are, feeling good about yourself, making smart decisions, and setting goals, (all topics in this book), are some of the foundational tools that you need to be successful in life.

I am a 21-year old senior at Georgia Institute of Technology in Atlanta, Georgia. Once I complete my studies, my long term goal, and ultimate career aspiration, is to open a preparatory school that focuses on technological global preparation for underprivileged children. The reason I'd like to do this is because of my experience in middle school and high school where I saw children struggling from a lack of guidance.

In my school (and several others I'm sure), the emphasis was placed on sports and not education. School had become a daycare, and many students were not being prepared for life after high school. More accurately, they weren't being prepared for a *successful* life after high school. Meanwhile, in some other countries, education is a top priority and students are reared as intellectuals and groomed for success.

Instead of playing the "blame game," and doing nothing, I developed a plan of action. I refuse to allow my situations and life circumstances to keep me from reaching out and helping all the students that I can. In order to do this, I must have a vision that students can be successful; I must have goals so that I will know what I'm reaching toward; I must persevere because it won't be easy.

One person can make a difference and change the world, and I challenge you to be that person. It is my hope that as you go through this book, you too will get the determination and courage to be a difference-maker, take a stand for what's important to you, and set yourself apart from the crowd.

As I continue my road map through life, the lessons I've learned from failures and mistakes will stay with me and aid me in achieving my ideals and aspirations. I feel as if I am now walking in the perfect plan that God has made for me, and I am much happier because of it. I hope my message blesses you as God and countless others have blessed me.

Cheering you on,
Tiffany B. Troutman

ACKNOWLEDGEMENTS

I would like to especially thank:

My mom, Dorothy Zeigler, who told me in so many words as a little girl that I could conquer the world;

Douglas Mincey, my husband, friend, and "better half" who supports my every dream;

Darius Anthony, a remarkable young man who contributed to this book;

Tiffany B. Troutman, a future phenomenal woman who wrote the Foreword to this book;

Marian Muldrow, Ed. S., who edited this manuscript;

The volunteers, organizations, and people who have given me their time, financial support, and resources over the years to help girls reach their full potential;

My "unofficial" mentors - other women who I look up to and who have inspired me to be great; and

All of the girls who have taken to heart and applied the principles of this book to their lives.

INTRODUCTION

IT STARTS IN THE MIND

After conducting numerous workshops and conferences for girls at schools, churches, community groups, and nonprofit organizations for many years, it became impressed upon me that more girls need to know who they are and how to reach their full potential. In order to expand my reach and to impact millions of girls around the world, I knew I had to write this book. What began as just programs for girls has evolved into "a new mindset for life" for both girls and women.

In my workshops with girls and women, I've asked them what they are made to be. Some have said that they are made to be a life changer, a leader, and more than what their parent's expect of them. Though the answers varied slightly, the point they made was still the same: They have more in them than they realize. So do you. You were put here on this earth for a purpose and are destined for greatness. By just changing your view of who you are, you can accomplish more than you imagined possible.

This book is about realizing your value as a young lady, reaching your potential as a woman, and maximizing your opportunities for a successful life. It's also about making wise choices and daring to be different from your peers. Lastly, it's about knowing deep down inside that you were created to be someone special and making up your mind to become that person. After all, you become what you think you are. It might seem like you're making the same mistakes or that it's taking you too long to make the progress you want. That's okay.

Let me tell you about Cindy. Cindy, an 8th grader, was in one of my in-school sessions for girls that lasted only a few weeks instead of months. At the end of the sessions, she sent an email thanking us for the program and stating that she didn't know how much it meant to tell herself every day that she is beautiful. Though Cindy did not go through a full semester of sessions, she understood and clung to the message that she received: She is beautiful. I call her a "sponge" because she soaked up every word and was very attentive. For her, that one message that she is beautiful could change her attitude, her decisions, and even her life.

On the other hand, I've seen girls who have gone through many months of sessions but did not change their behavior. Instead, they continued the same behavior that initially caused them problems. Though they were present for the lessons and even participated, for some reason, they did not strive to change their way of thinking.

My point is that sometimes it might take a person a long time to get the message that is intended for that individual, while at other times it might take only one session, one chapter, or one paragraph. If you have an open mind to the words in this book, you will understand the principles that apply to you and you will be able to apply them to your life.

As you proceed on your journey of becoming a woman, know that I am cheering you on all the way. Now turn the page, and get ready for your *new mindset for life.*

1

THERE'S MORE IN YOU

"Never underestimate the power of dreams and the influence of the human spirit. We are all the same in this notion: The potential for greatness lives within each of us."
~Wilma Rudolph (1940 - 1994)
First American woman runner to win three
gold medals at a single Olympics

I've met and talked to many girls through my line of work. Some of them have been bright, outgoing, and shined with confidence and others have been sad, withdrawn, and unsure of themselves. Some of them have been leaders, while still others have been followers. However, what they had in common was that they were young women who wanted love and acceptance. Don't you? I still do.

Several years ago, I saw two girls walking in my old neighborhood. They had on "short shorts" and shirts that left little to the imagination. I knew that they would attract attention from boys, but I also knew that it would be the wrong type of attention. I asked myself, do these girls think that this is the only way to meet a boy? Do they realize that they are intelligent and that their personality draws people to them? Do they even *know* what's inside of them? Do you?

Meet Karla. Karla was in middle school. She was a pretty girl by most people's definition. She was well-spoken and had the potential to be such a great leader, but she had a terrible habit of following others. She also had a bad reputation with boys and would get into fights with girls. In addition, she used language that was definitely not proper for a young lady.

When she joined ROTC at her high school, I was really excited for her. She looked like a professional young lady in her navy blue uniform and shiny, polished shoes. I was so impressed and proud of her! Needless to say, I was shocked when I heard that she was sent to an alternative school for threatening to physically harm another girl.

No matter how much I talked to her, Karla did not change her negative ways; instead, she seemed to get worse. As a matter of fact, she cussed so badly on Facebook that I had to block her from being my "friend." I know that Karla had family issues that probably contributed to her behavior, but I also believe that a big part of her problem was that she did not know that deep inside she was a very smart and powerful young lady who was born for a purpose. Her way of thinking, about life and herself, was not a positive one, and it showed in her behavior.

The potential for greatness lives within each of us.

Point 1: Don't Limit Yourself

I remember a time that I saw a caterpillar. I thought that it was just an unattractive, hairy worm that made my skin crawl. It was black, fat, short and moved slowly on the ground. Just by looking at it, I did not know that it was a creature that was created to be so much more. You see, a caterpillar has to go through a change in its life and when this change happens, the caterpillar becomes a beautiful butterfly with vibrant colors. Instead of crawling, it is now flying; instead of being limited to the ground, it can fly from flower to flower; instead of being unattractive, it is now a creature of beauty.

Like that caterpillar, at first glance, you might not think that you are beautiful. Maybe because of your circumstances, (you grew up without a father, you grew up in a group home, or you had a baby as a teenager), you might not think that you can accomplish your dreams. Perhaps no one gave you the confidence to do better. Or, perhaps you are doing well, but peer pressure, fear, or resources are holding you back from maximizing your potential.

Regardless of how your circumstances look, you have to understand that your circumstances do not define who you are. Since greatness is already in you, you don't have to try to become great. Like the caterpillar, you already have inside of you all that you need to be great. See yourself for who you really are: beautiful, divinely designed, and someone who is able to reach new heights.

Point 2: Average Is Not an Option

There is a saying that average is "the top of the bottom and the bottom of the top." Other words that are used to describe an average person are: *regular, normal, usual, typical, common,* or *ordinary.* Do these words describe you?

Average people just blend in the crowd and hardly get noticed. Some people are okay with that. They don't mind coming in second, third, or even last place. Or, they are fine with making a "C" in a class as long as they pass the class. This attitude may allow you to achieve some of your goals (discussed in Chapter 4) if you've set low goals for yourself. However, this carefree attitude will most likely stop you from being the best person you can be and excelling in life.

Hard work and sacrifice is rewarded. Laziness is not.

If you are running a race, why not train to win? If you are going to class, why not study, take notes, or even get tutored if it will help you to get an "A" out of the class. The point is that you should put your all in everything you do. Hard work and sacrifice is rewarded. Laziness is not.

Point 3: You are Full of Potential and Power

You are full of potential. This means that you have the capability (are able) to achieve greatness even at your age. Let's consider an orange. When you cut it open, it has many orange seeds (unless it's a seedless orange of course). Each seed has the power to grow an orange tree, and that orange tree produces more oranges with seeds. These seeds can then become orange trees and the process of multiplication continues. What does this have to do with you? Like the orange seed that continues to produce other oranges, you have the power to produce ideas that can change the world.

Let me illustrate. When you talk to your friend about the importance of making good grades or staying in school and she does it, your seeds of hope might have just encouraged her to become the next student body president or the president of the United States! Either way, they are both people of power and influence.

Don't sell yourself short. Your presence and your personality are unique and can help others accomplish their dreams. In addition, going after your own dreams can influence, inspire, and encourage others to accomplish their dreams. Be the best you can be and know that greatness is inside of you, and it is contagious – when people are around you, they can't help but be encouraged and grow. Unleash your potential. You never know who's watching you or what you'll accomplish.

Affirmation
"There is more to me than I realize, so I will try to live up to my potential."

Reflect

What does being "more" mean to you?

After you've reflected on this question, write your answer in the space below.

_____
_____
_____
_____
_____

Record

What five things are you "more than?" For example, "I am more than scared."

_____
_____
_____
_____
_____

Now, what five things are you made to be? This can be an adjective, such as, "I am made to be <u>awesome;</u>" or a noun, such as, "I am made to be <u>a leader;</u>" or a combination of both.

_____
_____
_____
_____
_____

Write an affirmation that Karla could say that might help her to change her behavior.

_____
_____
_____

Remark

The slogan for The RG Mincey Group is *"a new mindset for life."* What is a mindset and how does it apply to the title of this chapter, *"There is More in You?"*

_____
_____
_____
_____
_____
_____
_____
_____

Think about a time when you know you didn't do your best? Why didn't you do your best? What happened as a result?

_____
_____
_____
_____
_____
_____
_____
_____
_____

What is keeping you from living up to your full potential?

_____
_____
_____
_____
_____

Respond

What steps can you take to help you reach your full potential? When will you take these steps?

ACTION   **DATE**

_____
_____
_____
_____
_____

Rewrite the quote from the first page of this chapter in your own words.

_____
_____
_____
_____
_____
_____
_____
_____
_____
_____
_____
_____
_____
_____
_____
_____
_____
_____
_____
_____

I AM MADE TO BE MORE

I am fearfully and wonderfully made
to do good works that won't fade;
to show more excellence in all I do;
to have more success in all I pursue;
to give more time to those in need;
to do more for others in word and deed;
to love more and be selfless;
to strive for more and obtain the best.
I am made for more prosperity.
I am made for the greatness God's planned for me.
In my future, there's a lot in store
for I have purpose. I am made to be more.

Copyright 2012, Rhonda G. Mincey

2

YOU ARE UNIQUELY YOU

"One of the lessons that I grew up with was to always stay true to yourself and never let what somebody else says distract you from your goals. And so when I hear about negative and false attacks, I really don't invest any energy in them, because I know who I am."
~First Lady Michelle Obama (1964 -)

How do you feel about yourself? Are you confident or shy? Do you think that you are pretty or are you really hard on yourself? Have you been called fat and now you are dieting to lose weight? Do you laugh at the jokes that people make about you, but inside you are really crying? Do you bully others to feel powerful?

Self-esteem is the way you feel about yourself. You can have high self-esteem or low self-esteem. Many girls that I have met have low self-esteem, and some of them don't know it. However, it shows in the way that they dress, behave, and treat themselves and people around them.

I remember a girl I met named Tracy. Tracy was in middle school. Her classmates teased her because she talked "differently." Tracy had a very slight speech impediment that made her sound like she was from the Caribbean Islands when she spoke. When Tracy's mother introduced her to me, she walked slowly with her shoulders humped forward and her head held down. She was only thirteen years old, but the sadness in her face made her look older. She had bandages on her fingernails to prevent her from biting them because of the nervousness she felt about going to school. Even though she was an honor student, you would not know it by looking at her. My heart broke for Tracy, and I had mixed emotions. I wanted so badly to let her know that what the students said about her didn't matter, but it did matter to her. I also felt a sense of anger towards the kids at school who thought it was okay to tease her, not knowing or not caring about the effect it had on her.

I decided to spend time with Tracy and asked her about her experience at school. As I listened, I encouraged her and gave her a much needed heart-to-heart "pep-talk." She left my office about thirty minutes later feeling very confident. Her walk had changed (now she stood straight up), and she was engaging me in conversation, smiling, and even laughing! I could see a tremendous difference in her. For a few minutes, she appeared to believe in herself, and it showed.

If you believe in yourself, it is highly likely that other people will believe in you too! Don't listen to haters. If they are talking about you, it is because they are insecure in who they are. Have the mindset of First Lady Michelle Obama when she said, "...I know who I am." Then own it.

Point 1: You Become What You Think You Are

The mind is an amazing part of the body. It is where thoughts take place. When you think a certain way, you start to believe what you think. Then, you begin to *act* on what you think. For example, I remember when I decided to go to college after many years of being out of high school. Math was not my favorite subject because I could not understand why we had to put alphabets with numbers as we do in Algebra. How did this apply to real life anyway? Couldn't we just do addition and subtraction and call it a day? I had to take Algebra in college, so I decided that I would learn it and even like it! I told myself that I was smart, and I changed the way that I thought about numbers – instead of them being a scary foreign language to me, they were just inanimate numbers (and alphabets) on a page that could not think, but I could so I had the advantage.

Because I believed I was smart, I acted smart by studying often and asking for help. As a result, I got an "A" out of Algebra. I became what I thought I was, smart! Actually, I think that I was pretty smart to begin with, but I would let numbers intimidate me. However, when I deliberately *decided* that I was smart, I made excellent grades. I realized that once my mind was made to do something, I could do it and do it very well.

I suggest that you take note of your good qualities. Train your brain to think good things about you. Tell yourself that you are smart. Say it out loud right now. Tell yourself that you make good decisions. If there is something that you want to do and you don't think you can do it, you have to first believe that you can do it. Then you can begin taking the steps to get it done. See yourself accomplishing your goals, finishing school, travelling the world, writing your bestselling book, becoming an entrepreneur, or whatever it is that you'd like to do or become. There is nothing more powerful than a made up mind.

Accept, appreciate, and embrace your uniqueness.

Point 2: Don't Make Comparisons

How often have you seen someone and you compared yourself to him or her? Maybe it's a girl in your class or on television. Maybe it's your friend. When I was in my teens, I compared myself to other girls and sometimes was even jealous of them. Now that I am an adult, I realize that this is not wise to do.

Comparing yourself (your hair, your weight, your athletic ability, etc.), to someone else is unrealistic because you are a totally different person. Even if you have siblings from the same parents, you are still very different from each other. For example, I've seen brothers whose personalities are like night and day; one brother is very mild-mannered and easy going and the other brother is the total opposite – he cusses in everyday conversation and tells the truth about a person without thinking twice about how that person feels.

Comparing yourself to someone else is also like comparing apples and oranges. They are both fruit, but they are different *kinds* of fruit. So, they don't look alike, feel alike, or taste alike, nor should they. Why should an apple want to be orange when it is not made to be orange? It is made to be red, green, or yellow. If it were orange, it would not be an apple. If you had someone else's talents, complexion, or hair, then you would not be *you*.

Another reason you should not compare yourself to others is that it is unfair to yourself. When you compare yourself to someone else, you are measuring yourself against them. As a result, you might try to change your personality or your appearance to be like them. This is unfair to you because you are trying to be someone who you are not and will never be. This is like telling yourself over and over that you don't like *you*. Eventually, you will begin to dislike yourself, and it will show in the way that you treat yourself and allow others to treat you. Instead, be kind to yourself. Accept, appreciate, and embrace your own uniqueness. Remember that you are an original work of art.

Point 3: Be Your Own Best Friend

Who's your "BFF?" What is the difference between a friend and "best friend?" Do you have more than one best friend? If so, is one the "first" best friend and the other the "second" best friend? According to the world of social media, particularly Facebook, a friend can be anyone and is oftentimes a complete stranger. In this case, this is obviously not a *true* friend. A true friend is someone you are emotionally close with, someone you think well of, and who you defend or support even when your friend makes a mistake.

A *best* friend is usually one person among your other friends with whom you have the closest relationship. So, if you are *your* best friend, you should think good things about you; you can laugh at yourself; you have your "own back"; you defend your values and dreams; you can depend on you to be there for you; and you don't listen to negative talk about you. Just like you are honest with your best friend, be honest with yourself and accept you for who you are.

Affirmation
"Today I decide to love me just like I am, not to compare myself with anyone else, and give myself an "atta-girl."

Reflect

Why do people compare themselves with others?

_____
_____
_____
_____
_____
_____
_____

Record

1. How we see ourselves is usually reflected in our self-esteem. Draw a small picture of yourself. On one side of the picture, write down the qualities that you like about yourself. On the other side of the picture, write down some traits that could be improved upon.

2. Write an acrostic poem using the letters in your first name. Next to each letter, write a positive adjective that describes you. Then put it where you can see it daily. For example: KIM

K – Kind
I – Important
M – Magnificent

3. Write a short letter to Tracy to encourage her.

_____
_____
_____
_____
_____
_____
_____
_____
_____
_____
_____
_____
_____
_____
_____
_____
_____

Remark

What is the difference between high self-esteem and low self-esteem?

_____
_____
_____
_____
_____

When you make wise choices for yourself, how does that make you feel?

_____
_____
_____
_____

When you make really poor choices for yourself, how does that make you feel?
_____
_____
_____

When is the last time you spoke positively about yourself? What did you say? How did you feel?
_____
_____
_____
_____
_____
_____
_____

Respond

What steps can you take to help you think highly about yourself? When will you take these steps?

ACTION   **DATE**
_____
_____
_____
_____
_____

Rewrite the quote from the first page of this chapter in your own words.
_____
_____
_____
_____
_____

I LOVE ME

I love me with skinny legs and all
For it is these legs that have helped me climb
the ladder of success.
Will I appeal to someone any less?

I love me with my small little nose
for it is this nose that has smelled the rain
before it fell upon the earth.
After all, what is a pointy nose worth?

I love me with all my flaws.
For it is my flaws that remind me that I'm not perfect.
Instead, I'll use what I have and yes, I will work it!

I love me with my curly hair.
For it is this hair that can be braided, platted,
pinned up or worn in a fro.
Why did the texture of my hair once bother me so?

Yes, I am definitely different, uniquely me;
masterfully created, wholeheartedly free!
When you gaze my way, what do you see?

I can accept the person within;
the part of my soul where only few have been.
Are you my enemy or my friend?

The friend, the mirror, that when I gaze its way;
reaffirms that I'm okay
and that when my outer appearance fade
I am still wonderfully and fearfully made!

(Continued on next page)

Though you might laugh or disagree,
I am all that I am but not all I will be
because I've learned to love me, unashamedly.
Yes, I love me to the nth degree.

What is it about you that you haven't embraced?
Your small lips, wide hips, light skin, dark face?
Your walk, your talk, your personality?
When you look in the mirror, do you love what you see?
Or is it someone else that you long to be?

Don't dare compare yourself to me,
your friends, or even a celebrity.
For the people you see in videos or TV
are not all that they're made out to be.

So be true to you. To yourself, be true.
Let no one define our undermine you.
Love yourself with all your heart
because you are a work of art.

Copyright 2012, Rhonda G. Mincey

3

TAKE A STAND
By Darius Anthony

"If you don't stand for something, you'll fall for anything."
~Unknown

Have you ever been in a situation where you had to stand up for what was right? I am sure you will answer "Yes" to that question. It is not easy to stand up for what is right; especially when you have to stand up to your peers or someone you love and cherish. It is okay to admit that it is not easy to do because it is not easy for most people, but it has to be done.

Standards are internal rules that you tend to follow to help guide your behavior. These standard rules are not "set in stone," but we do tend to try to live by them every day—well, we should try to live by them every day. Values are what you consider most important in life. They are the things that really matter to us; the ideas and beliefs that we consider special. We tend to learn our values and standards at home, church, or even school.

Point 1: Maintain Your Values at All Times

Let's look at Steven as an example. Steven was a bright and intelligent individual. He was well-known around his school as the "smart guy." Not only was he smart, but he was very athletic. He played basketball, baseball and football. Since his ninth grade year, he was swamped by girls who wanted to date him—you know; he was the typical jock that we see in the movies and probably at your local school.

Steven made it all the way to his eleventh grade year with no problems, but at the end of his eleventh grade year, he started to slack in his work. He would barely do his homework, and he would seem to skip his Trig class. He did not care because he knew he was smart enough to get by without going to class. His parents had always taught him that he is to go to school every day, do his homework, and make the best of his time, but Steven had changed.

Steven's fame got to his head, and he decided that he could do what he wanted to do because he was Steven, "The Smart Guy." It just so happened that on one of the days Steven decided to skip his Trig class, his teacher gave a pop quiz—those quizzes that none of us like! Steven's teacher would not let him make it up because his absence was not an excused one; he didn't come to class. As a result, he received a zero for that quiz. Not only did he receive a zero for the quiz, he was suspended from two football games by his coach!

Values are what you consider most important in life.

In my honest opinion, I think that his suspension hurt him more than receiving the zero because he loved sports, especially football. It was his life, but his coach stated that he would not tolerate any of his student athletes skipping class and still being able to play in the games. Like I stated above, Steven was one of the best players on the team, so it hurt his coach to sit him out, but it taught Steven a lesson that he would never forget.

From that time forward, Steven decided that he would stick to his values and standards at all times and not allow his "friends" to steer him wrong. He had to stand up to them and let them know that his education was more important than them. He also had to take a stand and say that he would not be easily persuaded because he is well-known. I can tell this story because I witnessed it all—Steven is my cousin.

As you can see, Steven compromised his values and standards that were taught to him by his parents. Even so, he recognized his mistake of compromising his standards and values and took a stand against it. That made me proud of him.

Point 2: Recognize Your Mistakes and Take a Stand

It takes a big person to recognize that he or she has made a mistake and then fix it by taking a stand. It may seem as though this is not true, but everyone can take a stand. You cannot ever go back and fix a mistake because once it is made it is made, but you can start from where you are and work so you will not make that same mistake. That is taking a stand.

Taking a stand is not limited to a verbal stand. It could be by a change of actions, which in some circumstances is more important than speaking out against an issue. A person's words are null and void without action to support them.

A person's words are null and void without action.

If you have ever compromised your standards and values that you learned, do not feel bad because you are not the only one. Just do better. Now that you know better, you have the ability to take a stand and say "not another time will I compromise my values and standards." That's exactly what Steven did, as mentioned in the first point of this chapter. He recognized that he messed up. In fact, he suffered consequences for compromising his values and standards—he failed the quiz. Even though he failed, he still took a stand and declared that he would not do it again. That is the same way you have to act in every situation. Take a stand!

You may have made plenty of mistakes, but you do not have to make the same mistake over and over. Stand up, hold your head up high, and declare that you will not compromise your standards and values again.

Point 3: Set Your Standards Early

Decide early in life what you value and what you will stand for. Then, when it's time to make decisions (Chapter 4), it will be easier to know what you *should* do, even if you don't always do that. Think of why we have traffic rules: If drivers do not have to obey the "rules of the road," they could just run red lights, cross the center line, and park wherever they wanted. This conduct would probably lead to people getting in accidents, getting into fights, or even getting seriously hurt. Therefore, the "rules of the road" are in place to give drivers guidance on where they can and cannot go and what they can and cannot do while driving.

Likewise, your standards should guide and protect you. If you haven't decided what you stand for, you will have no pre-determined standard to help you make a sound decision when that time comes. As a result, you will probably not make the best decision for you at that moment.

For example, if you decide that it is important to you for a guy to respect you, and one day he talks badly to you or even hits you, you will know that his action is totally unacceptable to you, and you can give him his walking papers. I've seen so many older girls who will date any guy who talks smoothly to them even though he is unemployed and does not have a GED. Make your mind up now that this will not be you.

Don't lower your standards to meet someone else's low standard. Bring that person up to your high standards. If a guy cannot or is unwilling to be the young man you need him to be, for whatever reason, drop him like a hot potato and move on! Don't waste your time trying to change him and reacting emotionally. Set your standards today about what matters to you, such as, your education, family, career, and a mate. This is worth saying twice: Don't lower your standards to meet other people's standards. Bring them up to yours!

Affirmation
"From now on, I declare that I will take a stand, and I will not compromise the standards and values that have been instilled in me."

Reflect

DO YOU THINK THAT YOU ARE ABLE TO TAKE A STAND TO SUPPORT YOUR STANDARDS AND VALUES?

To help you find out, start with the questions:
- ➢ Do I value what I have been taught or what I know is right?
- ➢ Am I willing to follow what I've been taught?
- ➢ Do I believe that taking a stand will make me a better person?

Record

After you've reflected on these questions, write your thoughts in the spaces below and on the next page:

_____
_____
_____
_____
_____
_____
_____
_____
_____
_____

What advice would you give someone who is having trouble taking a stand?

_____
_____
_____
_____
_____

Has there been a time when you went against your values? How did that make you feel? What did you learn?
_____
_____
_____
_____
_____

Remark

What do you value? For example, having integrity (not cheating or lying and keeping your word) or making good grades.
_____
_____
_____
_____

Is it difficult to have friends who don't value what you value? Why or why not?
_____
_____
_____
_____
_____
_____
_____
_____

What do values have to do with making choices?
_____
_____
_____
_____
_____

What should you consider when taking a stand?

Respond

What steps can you take to help you take a stand for what you believe? When will you take these steps?

ACTION   **DATE**

_____
_____
_____
_____
_____

Rewrite the quote from the first page of this chapter in your own words.

_____
_____
_____
_____
_____
_____
_____
_____
_____
_____
_____
_____
_____
_____
_____
_____
_____

STAND STRONG

Though peer pressure surrounds me everywhere I turn
and temptation's all around me, there's a lesson to be learned:

I can stand on my own and not follow the crowd;
make my own decisions and make myself proud.

I can say "NO" to things that are not good for me
and not worry about my status or popularity.

I can walk away before trouble begins
and listen to that voice within.

For, if other people's standards are lower than mine
I will leave them alone and be just fine.

And if our values do not match,
I can walk away gladly without looking back.

Because I know that what is in me
is more than they care to see.
The truth of the matter is that
my morals belong only to me.

And when people try to degrade or persuade me
I rely on the power of the One who made me.

So I will stand against what is wrong
Because I know I am not alone.

Copyright 2012, Rhonda G. Mincey

4
MAKE SMART DECISIONS

"Somewhere along the line of development we discover what we really are, and then we make our real decision for which we are responsible. Make that decision primarily for yourself because you can never really live anyone else's life, not even your own child's."
~ Eleanor Roosevelt (1884 - 1962)
Former First Lady of the United States

Every day you make countless decisions. A decision is making your mind up about an issue after considering the possible choices. Some of the decisions that you might make are so small that you might not realize that you are even making decisions. Some decisions happen so quickly that they seem to be automatic while others happen more deliberately and require more thought and time.

For example, did you brush your teeth today or put on deodorant? If so, you probably didn't have to put much thought into that. On the other hand, if you are considering what to wear to a party, you will probably think about this a little longer. Other decisions you might make are: How will you wear your hair? What time should you study? How long should you study? Should you give a boy your phone number? Will you try out to be a cheerleader? Will you cheat on a test? Will you join a school club? Will you go to college?

One of the most important decisions that you can make is who you let in your inner circle, date, and marry because people who are close to you have the power to influence you.

For example, if you decide to be friends with or date someone who doesn't have decent moral values and respectable character traits, you will more than likely regret that decision. Another important decision for you to make concerns your virginity. Deciding to have sex before you are married is a major decision, and it comes with serious, lasting, and "grown-up" consequences that you are just not emotionally prepared to handle. Don't give in to peer pressure or believe that having sex with a guy is the way to get him or keep him. Every girl is *not* "doing it," and you can set yourself apart by holding on to what should be precious to you and reserved for only your husband. If you have already engaged in sexual activity, it is not too late for you to decide to become abstinent. It may be difficult, but it has many benefits. Plus, you are worth the wait.

> The person in your inner circle can affect your life.

Decision-making is a very important part of life so you should consider all of the options before you make an important decision. If a decision is difficult, consider asking your parents or an older person you trust for advice. Also, don't make a hasty decision – take time to think about the *best* choice even if it takes a few days or weeks to do so.

Point 1: Today's Decisions Will Affect Your Future

The decisions you make today will affect where you will be tomorrow. For example, if you decide to drop out of school today, chances are that you will not get a "good" job unless you go back to school and get your high school diploma or GED, to start. Then you should consider getting your bachelor's and master's degrees also. Depending on the type of work you'd like to do, getting a doctorate degree might be beneficial. I am not saying that going to college is for every person; many people have done very well without doing so. However, I am a big fan of getting an education because it can give you opportunities, options, and access.

When you are educated, you have more opportunities to explore various career choices than you have with very little education. You also have more job options available to you with the more education you have. An education can also give you access to people you might not meet otherwise, who can possibly help you further your career or dream.

For example, my associate's degree opened doors for me. With that degree, I was able to become a substitute teacher, which gave me the opportunity to have access to teachers who could help me with my passion to help girls. Another example is that while I was getting my bachelor's degree, I met several professors who were instrumental in helping me to reach some important personal goals. In addition, my decision to go back to school gave me the confidence and knowledge that I apply to my business and personal life. That decision has helped me to get where I am today.

> Education can give you opportunities, options, and access.

I know a young man, Tommy, who decided to drop out of high school. Hanging with the wrong crowd, he became rebellious and joined a gang. Tommy was eventually put out of his parent's house. In time, he lived on the streets, and was unwelcomed in his own parents' home until he changed his unruly behavior. A year later, he was in jail for assault.

When Tommy made the decision to drop out of school and hang with his "friends," it affected his life a year later, and still does to this day. His relationship with his parents is strained and may be difficult to repair. Doing what is right is still a constant struggle for Tommy, but he understands where his rebellious behavior got him.

In Tommy's situation, his poor decisions had many negative consequences. Likewise, if a person makes wise decisions early in life, chances are greater that he or she will be successful later in life.

A saying that I have found to be true is: If you fail to plan, you plan to fail. To illustrate that, let's say that you plan to become a lawyer. In order to make that happen, you have to decide as soon as possible what steps you need to take to make your dream come true (Chapter 6), then put the plan into action. Since you need to graduate from college to attend law school, you would be wise to be sure that you do all that you can to graduate from high school. This includes taking simple steps, such as, going to school, obeying the rules, and making passing grades, at a minimum. If not, you are planning to fail.

> Make wise decisions early in life.

Judge Judy or Judge Hatchett did not become a judge overnight. They made several smart decisions a long time ago to get where they are today. As a result, they are very successful and influential women.

Point 2: Every Decision Has Consequences

Every decision, when acted on, has a consequence and some decisions have *several* consequences. A consequence is simply a result that occurs because an action has been taken. For instance, if you study and prepare for an exam, you will probably get a good grade. The consequence of your studying is that you get an "A" or a "B" and that you are elated that your hard work paid off. On the flip side, let's say that you decide not to brush your teeth after every meal. As a result, you might have to get some teeth pulled, you might develop gum disease, or you might need fillings. Either way, these results are direct consequences to your decision not to brush your teeth.

Some consequences will be seen immediately (right after the decision is made) while other consequences won't be seen until further down the road. For example, when you study and take a test, your results are usually given to you relatively soon. You get your test paper returned or log on the computer and see your grade. However, in the above scenario about neglecting to brush your teeth, the results are typically not seen or felt until quite some time. Eventually, your toothache lets you know that you need to see a dentist. Your dentist then tells you that you have a cavity that took some time to develop and could have been prevented.

Point 3: Some Decisions are Life-Changing

Some decisions that you make have "life-changing" consequences and other decisions may not have a major impact on your life. For instance, failing a class can greatly affect your life, but is it "life-changing?" If failing a class means that your grade point average is too low for you to graduate, and this failure could directly affect the amount of money you make and the career path you choose, then the answer could be yes. On the other hand, if it means that you have to repeat the class during the summer, then the answer is probably no. Either way, sometimes we do not understand the full effect of our decisions until later in life when it is difficult and sometimes impossible to undo the consequences.

I know a young girl named Cynthia. Cynthia is a very pretty girl, who is also very smart and talented. However, she has a pattern of making very poor decisions. She lost her virginity at the age of thirteen. She eventually graduated from high school and began college. During this time, she saw her old boyfriend and dropped out of college at the age of nineteen to follow him to another city, against her parents' wishes. The boyfriend sells drugs and occasionally hits Cynthia, but she denies it. Even so, she is still with him.

He moved into her apartment with her, and she pays the bills. Now she is pregnant by him, and he is in and out of jail. She had planned to go into the military, but now that she's pregnant, that is no longer an option for her. Her decision to become a mother is life-changing. Her life will never be the same, and she now has to think about her baby in every decision that she makes. She is now working and in school but hardly has any money left after she gets paid. To make matters worse, her boyfriend is seeing other girls. Cynthia's life didn't have to be this way because both her parents love her and gave her proper guidance. However, because she chose not to listen to them, her life has changed forever.

Everyone's situation is different and girls behave in certain ways for different reasons. However, regardless of the situation, consequences are real and some of them will change your life forever, sometimes positively and other times negatively. In the next chapter, we'll see the role that making smart decisions play in dealing with pressures that you might face.

Affirmation
"Today I decide to make good decisions about what I do and who I am with because these decisions will affect my future."

Reflect

WHY IS IT DIFFICULT FOR SOME PEOPLE TO MAKE SMART DECISIONS?

To help you find out, start with the questions:
- ❖ Do I have the right people around me to help me make smart decisions?
- ❖ Am I pressured by me peers to make decisions that are bad for me?
- ❖ Do I make bad decisions for myself because I can "get away with it?"

Record

After you've reflected on these questions, write your thoughts in the space below:

_____
_____
_____
_____
_____
_____
_____
_____
_____
_____

Think about some decisions that you wish you *did not* make. How did those decisions make you feel? Will you make those same decisions again? Why or why not? Write about it.

_____
_____
_____
_____
_____
_____

Think about some decisions that you are *glad* you made. How did those decisions make you feel? Why or why not? Write about it.

_____
_____
_____
_____
_____
_____
_____
_____
_____
_____
_____

The decisions you make can affect other people. List two decisions that you have made and how they have affected *other people* besides you.

_____
_____
_____
_____
_____
_____
_____
_____
_____
_____
_____
_____
_____

Remark

What is a negative or positive consequence that can result from the following decisions? List at least two.

Graduate from high school

_____
_____
_____
_____

Get a college degree (bachelor's, master's or doctorate's degree)

_____
_____
_____
_____

Have sex before you get married

_____
_____
_____
_____

Lie to your parents

_____
_____
_____
_____

Talk back or disobey people in authority

_____
_____
_____
_____

Drop out of school

_____
_____
_____

Date someone who verbally or physically abuses you

_____
_____
_____

Bully someone

_____
_____
_____

Drink alcohol (beer and liquor)

_____
_____
_____

Exercise three to five days a week

_____
_____
_____

Avoid exercising

_____
_____
_____

Smoke cigarettes, use tobacco or drugs, including marijuana
_____
_____
_____
_____

Save 10% of your salary or allowance
_____
_____
_____
_____

Start your own business
_____
_____
_____
_____
_____

Volunteer for a cause you believe in
_____
_____
_____
_____

Get pregnant before you are married
_____
_____
_____
_____

Cheat on a test or homework
_____
_____
_____
_____

Respond

What steps can you take to help you make wise decisions? When will you take these steps?

ACTION   **DATE**

_____
_____
_____
_____
_____

Rewrite the quote from the first page of this chapter in your own words.

_____
_____
_____
_____
_____
_____
_____
_____
_____
_____
_____
_____
_____
_____
_____
_____
_____
_____
_____

CHOICES

Every choice I make has a consequence
So, when I choose, I use common sense.

I also must decide what is best for me
and make the decision with accountability.

The results of my decisions can cause joy or pain.
So, I have to ask the question: What will I lose or gain?

Who, besides me, will my decisions affect?
Will it give me a life of promise, or one of regret?

The decisions I make today will affect each tomorrow.
The consequence will lead to success or sorrow.

So, I will choose to be smart. I choose to work hard.
I choose to be my "best" me; of drugs I'll have no part.

I choose to have a positive attitude.
I choose not to drink alcohol, which can alter my mood.

I chose not to smoke cigarettes to relieve my stress.
I choose to make A's and B's and not "just pass" a test.

I choose to honor my body, and not give in to sex
for that gift is for my spouse and I know that it is best.

When I decide to do something whether it's right or wrong,
I must accept the consequences, for they are mine alone.

So, today I decide at this very hour
to choose the best path for me, for only I have that power.

Copyright 2012, Rhonda G. Mincey

5
PRESSURES DON'T HAVE TO CRUSH YOU

"Be of good cheer. Do not think of today's failures, but of the success that may come tomorrow. You have set yourselves a difficult task, but you will succeed if you persevere; and you will find a joy in overcoming obstacles. Remember, no effort that we make to attain something beautiful is ever lost."
~ Helen Keller (1880 - 1968)
Author, political activist, and lecturer

Life is filled with pressures, and most people feel the weight of being pressured from time to time. We often hear about "peer pressure," but exactly what does "pressure" mean? For this chapter, pressure has two definitions: *a state of worry and urgency,* such as when you are running late for a job interview; and *to apply great pressure or a strong influence on somebody in order to force him or her to do something.* For example, you might feel the pressure to smoke with your friends or co-workers or even to bully a student.

Pressures can be divided into internal pressures (the pressures you put on yourself) and external pressures (the pressures that other people put on you – usually your peers).

Point 1: Pressures are Common

Both girls and boys encounter pressures through their teenage years. Some girls experience the pressure of being popular, being thin, or trying out for a team sport. Other girls might feel the pressure of engaging in risky behaviors like drinking alcohol, having sex before marriage, using drugs, and even getting pregnant. Still some girls feel the pressure of making the honor roll, getting into college, or making their parents proud.

As a young girl, I experienced the pressures to try drugs, have sex, and skip school. I typically didn't give in to peer pressure because I thought about what my mother would do to me if I got caught; plus, I didn't want to disappoint her, but I sure was tempted by my peers as are most teens. To help me deal the with pressures of being a teenager, I associated with two other girls who thought like me so that helped me to stay out of trouble. Even then, sometimes it was not easy to resist the temptation to go places where we should not have gone or to stay out past curfew.

Like girls, boys also deal with many pressures. They might be pressured into joining a gang, wearing a certain brand of clothes, being the "man" of the house because their father is not there, excelling in sports, "snitching" on a friend, or having sex with as many girls as they can when they are not ready or it goes against what they believe. I see many boys giving into the pressure of wearing certain brands of clothing to impress others even when their parents can't afford them or when it means making another young man feel that he doesn't measure up to his peers.

Believe it or not, adults feel the pressures of life also.

When you become an adult, pressures do not stop. Believe it or not, adults feel the pressures of life also. Some adults worry about doing well on their job, finding a job, taking care of their children, earning enough money to support their family, having a close relationship with their spouse, getting a divorce, being accepted by their neighbors, and dealing with problems at home, just to name a few. As an adult, one of the pressures I dealt with while writing this book is excelling in college. This is pressure that I put on myself because I want to be the best at what I do, but I am glad to say that I have made straight A's for almost four years! Even so, I have to outweigh the stress and sacrifice against the rewards. Though it might seem that pressures can last almost a lifetime, it is reassuring to know that the pressures you experience don't have to crush you, and that some of them can even make you a better person.

Point 2: Pressures can be Positive

Pressure can bring about stress (one way the body reacts to pressure), anxiety, and worry. A certain amount of stress is normal, but stress can be harmful when the body doesn't get rid of it in a healthy way, such as in exercising, meditating, or listening to music that relaxes you.

However, all pressure is not negative and can even help develop your character. For instance, when you encounter someone who is pressuring you to do what you believe is wrong, or when you have a situation that makes you feel stressed, you have to decide how to respond. When you respond appropriately, you begin to realize "what you're made of."

Let's say that you feel pressured to cheat on an important test because you didn't study. You realize that you could fail the class if you are caught cheating on the test. More importantly, cheating just doesn't feel right to you. So, instead of cheating, you say a prayer or cross your fingers, do the best you can on the test, and vow that the next time you will be sure to study ahead of time. While you might not have made your *best* grade, you can look yourself in the mirror and smile knowing that you were honest.

With each positive response (every time you don't give into the pressure), you lay the foundation that will develop your character and help you continue to do what is right. This increases your self-esteem, and you become more confident in your ability to handle pressures in the right way.

In addition to bringing out the best in a person, pressure can also bring out the brilliance in an object. Consider the diamond. A diamond is usually given to someone on special occasions, such as, an engagement, birthday, or wedding anniversary. A diamond also signifies love and importance and is said to be a "girl's best friend."

According to the Gemological Institute of America,

- ❖ A diamond is the most durable gemstone and is considered to be the hardest natural substance on earth.
- ❖ Diamonds are virtually fireproof.
- ❖ A diamond is formed approximately 100 miles from the earth's surface.
- ❖ Diamonds come to the earth's surface by being pushed through the earth through volcanic activity.

Pressure has a way of making you shine like a diamond!

Talk about pressure! Without that pushing movement, we would not be able to admire a diamond for its many qualities and it would not be the symbol of love and success that it is known for. Like a diamond, you are tough, precious, desirable, valuable, unbreakable and fireproof!

The circumstances of your life takes you through a process that is not always easy, but this helps you to become your "true you." Like a diamond, pressure has a way of making you shine even through the toughest circumstances and darkest places of your life.

Point 3: You Can Handle Pressures

We've discussed some of the many types of pressures that you might face, but how do you handle those pressures without letting them get the best of you? First of all, when you are facing *external* pressures, such as a friend trying to get you to lie to your parents about where you are going, know what you stand for and what your values are (Chapter 3). This way, it will be easier for you to take a stand and say, "No" because you've already decided what you will and will not do. Also, you have to consider and understand the *consequences* of your decision to give in to peer pressure and go against your values (Chapter 4).

Next, use your voice. This means, saying, "No." "No" isn't a dirty word. Saying the word "No" to your peers takes courage, but it can save you from terrible consequences. Remember this: People who try to persuade you to participate in behaviors that you feel uncomfortable doing or that are wrong do not have your best interest in heart. They also are not your friends, and probably do not think highly of you, so you don't have to impress them. In a few years, you might not even remember their name.

If someone is pressuring you into doing activities that goes against your values, such as smoking, using drugs, drinking alcohol, having sex, dropping out of school, lying to someone, cheating on a test, or engaging in illegal behavior, ask yourself these seven questions:

1. How will it affect my future?
2. How will it affect my family?
3. How will it affect my health?
4. How will it affect my reputation?
5. How will I feel about myself afterwards?
6. Would I want my little brother or little sister to see me do this?
7. If my mother or someone else I respect was with me now, would I do this?

Now let's say that you're faced with *internal* pressures, like getting a job promotion or becoming the first person in your family to graduate from college. There are several steps that you can take in order to lessen the pressure on you. A few of them are listed below:

- Learn your limits. Set realistic goals about what you can achieve and how you will achieve it (Chapter 6).
- Ask yourself, "What is the absolute worst thing that can happen if I don't succeed?"
- Exercise to help relieve tension and stress and to clear your mind.
- Surround yourself with people who support you (friends, parents, teachers, etc.). Talk to them.
- Be your best friend and not your worst enemy. Do your best but don't take yourself too seriously.

Affirmation
I will not give in to the weight of pressures because I have the power to handle them.

Reflect

Do you ever put pressure on yourself by comparing yourself to others or by wanting to please others? Explain.

_____
_____
_____
_____
_____

Record

Write about pressures you feel as a daughter, student, and friend?

_____
_____
_____
_____
_____
_____
_____
_____

How do you know when pressures are getting to be too much for you to handle? What do you do then?

_____
_____
_____
_____
_____
_____
_____
_____

How do you deal with pressures? Can you think of a better way to handle them, or are you satisfied with the way you deal with them?

___

Remark

In what way does pressure affect the way you make choices? Are most of the pressures you feel *internal* or *external*?

___

Explain how pressure can produce a positive outcome. Have you experienced a positive consequence that came from pressure?

___

Diamonds come from pressure. Name three characteristics of diamonds. Can you apply them to you? How?

_____
_____
_____
_____
_____
_____
_____

Respond

What are some steps you can take to help you cope with pressures? When will you take these steps? (Think about what you can do and who you can reach out to for help).

ACTION   **DATE**

_____
_____
_____
_____
_____
_____
_____

Rewrite the quote from the first page of this chapter in your own words.

_____
_____
_____
_____
_____
_____
_____
_____

PRESSURES

Make good grades. Try out for track.
Do my chores and do not slack.

Study for the C.R.C.T.
Go to college. Get my G.E.D.

History or Biology?
Why is my mom yelling at me?

Will he call me? Will I win?
Will I have to take this test again?

Do I take Algebra or Trig?
Long or short? Weave or wig?

If he calls, what do I say?
When will this zit go away?

Want to smoke? No, I'm good,
but yet I wonder if I should.

Should I tweet? Where should we meet?
A pop quiz! Should I cheat or try to compete?

Decisions. Pressures. Noise. Fuss.
How do I cope without getting crushed?

I feel overwhelmed, tired and stressed
and yet I try to do my best,

but how do I cope with life's daily demands?
Please answer me if you can.

Copyright 2012, Rhonda G. Mincey

6

DREAM IT. DO IT!

"I want to be the drum major for my high school band, because it represents the crème de la crème (best of the best)."
~ Tiffany B. Troutman (1990 -)
College Honor Student

The above quote was from a teenager who spoke at a few of my events on the subject of Goal Setting. I was very impressed by her then, and now, at 21 years old, she continues to impress me and make me proud.

SUCCESS
Just Ahead

Tiffany is currently a senior at Georgia Institute of Technology in Atlanta, Georgia. Who better to make such a quote than a young woman who has accomplished so much, including being the Finance Committee Chair of Georgia Institute of Technology's Black Leadership Conference, as well as being a member of the Georgia Institute of Technology National Society of Black Engineers? (You may read more of Tiffany's thoughts in the Foreword of this book).

In order for you to accomplish what you set out to do, it is important to set a goal. A goal is simply an aim. For example, when I was in high school, one of my goals was to graduate from high school, which I did. When I began writing this book, one of my goals was to complete it and get it into schools across the U.S. I have had several goals across my lifetime, and you will too.

When Tiffany set her short term and long term goals, she applied an acronym that she learned while she was in the high school band: PRIDE, which stands for:

Perseverance – pressing on when the workload is heavy

Respect – consideration for peers, leaders, and yourself

Integrity – being honest in school and in the workplace

Discipline – doing what you must do even when you don't feel like it

Excellence – by applying all of the acronyms, you can achieve excellence in any situation

Point 1: Go for the Goal

Accomplishing goals require some effort, but it is worth the effort you put into it in the end. To help you accomplish a goal, you must first decide what is your goal? Do you want to be on a dance team? Do you want to make the honor roll? Is becoming a doctor a dream of yours?

Now that you've decided on your goal, you should take the necessary steps to help you reach it.

The first step is to write down your goal. When you write down your goal, you transfer your idea from your head to paper and make the goal real. You can see it!

The second step is to outline the steps to achieve your goal.

The third step is to set deadlines for reaching your goals. Be realistic when you are setting your deadlines so that you aren't disappointed. A calendar or chart can help you meet your deadlines.

The fourth step is to consider all of the possible obstacles and ways of handling them. When you have a goal, you will most likely have problems that can sidetrack you or even keep you from reaching your goal. Who or what might prevent you from reaching your goal? What are some potential problems that you might encounter? For instance, do you need money to help your start a dance company or private school? Do you have the wrong friends who might discourage you? Do you procrastinate (wait to do later what you can do now)?

The fifth step is to tell someone you trust about your goal. This person can help keep you on track and encourage you to reach your goal. Be careful to choose this person wisely because this is your "cheerleader." Choosing someone who is negative, jealous, or unsupportive is not a good idea so "guard your heart."

The last step is to put your steps into action. Believe in you. Make it happen, step by step, day by day.

Tell someone who believes in you about your goal.

As you go through these steps, it is important to have a positive outlook. Your mind is very powerful so envision yourself accomplishing your goal. See yourself in a positive light and as a success. Also, persevere. This means do not give up! You have to remain focused on your goal regardless of the obstacles that come your way. You might become discouraged or tired from trying to reach your goal, but if you want to cross the finish line, you have to remain in the race, and keep your eyes on the prize.

Point 2: What You See is What You'll Become

When you see an object, a picture is ingrained in your brain of that object or that event. It isn't enough to just *say* you have a goal; you have to *see* the goal. Once you write down (or draw) your goal, be sure to place it where you can see it as a reminder to you. You can place it in your locker at school, on your bathroom mirror, on your bedroom door or ceiling, in your car, or on your cell phone, for example. Keep it visible.

A dream board is an excellent visual reminder of your dream (what you'd like to do or be). A dream board is a collection of words and pictures that you creatively put together so that you can see what you'd like to accomplish. Making a dream board is easy to do. You will need:

1 Poster board
Scissors
Magazines
Glue sticks or tape
Sheet of paper or index cards
Markers, ink pen, or colored pencils

4 Steps to Making Your Dream Board

1. Visualize and write down what you'd like to accomplish or where you'd like to go, using words, such as college, car, Paris, Fashion Designer, etc.
2. Look through magazines or search on the Internet to find words or pictures that match your words in step 1.
3. Cut the pictures or words out and attach them to the poster board with glue sticks or tape.
4. Hang or place the poster board where you can see it daily.

Whether you write down your dream on a sheet of paper or make a dream board, an important point to remember is this: If you can see it, you can be it.

Point 3: Dream Big

If you're going to spend the time setting goals to accomplish a dream of yours, you might as well dream big! If you can imagine it, you can achieve it. Sure, it will take hard work and sacrifice but as my mother told me, "nothing worth having comes easy." For example, I am constantly continuing my education and one of my goals is to graduate at the top of my class – not just to "pass classes to graduate." So, I discipline myself to study to make good grades. I view it this way: If I have to put some time into my class to get a "C," I might as well put a little more effort in it to get an "A".

Another example is, when I began writing this book, I did not have a clear goal on how many books I wanted to sell. Well, I do now. I figure if I can sell a hundred books then why not sell a thousand, and if I can sell a thousand books, why not sell a million of them! Many of people have done it before, so why not me? Also, why limit the book to just the English language? If I want girls across the globe to read this book, I could have it translated into Spanish, French, and other languages.

The point is that if you think small, you will probably obtain small successes, but if you think big, you have the capacity to reach for and receive enormous, almost unimaginable successes. Sometimes our small thinking limits our potential and impact on others to accomplish great achievements.

Affirmation
"Today I will take the limits off of my dreams and dream big."

Reflect

If you could accomplish your wildest dream without worrying about money, what would you do?

_____
_____
_____
_____
_____

Record

Think of and write down one goal that you'd like to reach in the next six months, year, and five years. These must be goals that are important to you and are attainable. For each one, describe what you'll need to do in order to reach your goal. (Refer to the steps to setting and reaching goals in Point 1 of this chapter).

In six months I'd like to accomplish:
_____
_____
_____
_____
_____

In one year I'd like to accomplish:
_____
_____
_____
_____
_____
_____

In five years I'd like to accomplish:

_____
_____
_____
_____
_____
_____

Think of a person who has reached his or her goal. This person could be someone you know personally, someone you admire on television, or someone in history. Write a letter to him or her.

_____
_____
_____
_____
_____
_____
_____
_____
_____
_____
_____
_____
_____
_____
_____
_____
_____
_____
_____
_____
_____
_____

Remark

Why is it important to set goals?

_____
_____
_____
_____
_____
_____

How do you decide what your goals are?

_____
_____
_____
_____
_____

Is it better to set lower goals than to risk failure by setting higher ones? Why or Why not?

_____
_____
_____
_____
_____
_____
_____
_____

Have you had a "big" dream and did you go after it? What happened?

_____
_____
_____
_____

Have you taken a risk of failure to achieve a goal? What happened? Are you glad you took that risk?
_____
_____
_____
_____
_____
_____

What's the difference in failing and being a failure?
_____
_____
_____
_____
_____
_____

If you don't reach your goals are you a failure? Why or why not?
_____
_____
_____
_____
_____
_____

What are some positive ways to deal with disappointments?
_____
_____
_____
_____
_____
_____
_____
_____

What is meant by *"guard your heart"* in Point 2?

_____
_____
_____
_____
_____

How do you define success?

_____
_____
_____
_____
_____

How can using the acronym PRIDE help you to reach your goal?

_____
_____
_____
_____
_____

Respond

What steps can you take to help you reach your goals? When will you take these steps? (What date?)

ACTION	**DATE**
_____	_____
_____	_____
_____	_____
_____	_____
_____	_____

Rewrite the quote from the first page of this chapter in your own words.

_____
_____
_____
_____
_____
_____
_____
_____
_____
_____
_____
_____
_____
_____
_____
_____
_____
_____
_____
_____
_____
_____
_____
_____
_____
_____
_____

Make a dream board. Put it where you can see it every day.

I DARE YOU

Dare to dream ~
The dream that births opportunities.
The dream that leaves legacies
where you're the essence of royalty;
then, wake up and make it a reality.

Dare to soar ~
Soar higher and faster than you have before
with a wind force that no one can ignore;
Above pettiness and the world's affairs
– a place where you know that someone cares.

Dare to be different ~
Different from the models in the magazines
where your image is, many times, borderline obscene.
Recognize that it's not your genes but your mentality
that makes you a king or queen.

Dare to make choices ~
Choices that inspire, not kill;
choices that give life and heal;
choices that build and don't destroy;
choices that yield an unspeakable joy.

What is the dream that's been burning in you?
What is the thing that's been purposed for you?
What is the one thing you've been told you can't do?
That might be the dream you make come true.

(Continued on next page)

So dream! Soar! Be different!
Don't be dismayed by the days you've spent
settling for second and indecision.
Make your dream come into fruition.

Some of the greatest things you've heard or seen
have been done by people who've dared to dream.

So, go ahead. Dream! Push! Pursue!
Show me the power of what a made up mind can do.
And see for yourself that your dream can come true.
I dare you to dream. I double-dog dare you.

Copyright 2012, Rhonda G. Mincey

7

WOULD YOU FOLLOW YOU?
By Darius Anthony

"If your actions inspire others to dream more, learn more, do more and become more, you are a leader."
~John Quincy Adams (1767 - 1848)
Sixth President of the United States

At the age that you are now, it is so important to be a leader. Peer pressure can be a common experience for you. As I'm sure you know, it is very easy to get caught in a situation that would cause you to step out of your leadership role.

I would describe a leader as a person who does not succumb to peer pressure, a person who can make wise and sound decisions, and a person who is sure that he or she is a leader (confident) and will not purposely lead someone down the wrong path.

Being a leader does not mean you cannot follow someone. Being a leader simply means that you have the ability to resist peer pressure to do wrong, and you are able to lead if you have to do so. I consider myself as a leader, and I still follow other leaders.

Point 1: Lead by Example

What does it mean to lead by example? Leading by example simply means that you will demonstrate a specific behavior rather than just talking about it and not following it yourself. I know you've seen plenty of people who offer advice to others, but they do the opposite of what they tell others to do. I know because I used to be a person like that. I would tell a person to do this and do that, but I would not do it myself. I realized that people were not taking me seriously anymore, and they did not value what I was saying. As a result, I changed my actions and started to become a positive example. I also asked myself this question many times: "Would I follow me?" You must ask yourself that same question. If the answer to that question is "No," then no one else will follow you.

> At the age that you are now, it is so important to be a leader.

Tina, a very beautiful girl, was the hall monitor in school. She was always on her job; you could never get by Tina without your hall pass. She was tough, and she did not let anybody get by! If you were caught outside of your classroom without a hall pass, Tina would write you up for detention, no matter if you were her brother, sister or friend! She was just that serious about her job.

One day, Tina was outside of her class without a hall pass, and she received detention for not following the rules of the school. You can bet your $5 that the ENTIRE school found out because news travels fast in a high school. Tina was so ashamed and embarrassed that she had to go to detention, which is understandable because she was always making sure others followed the rules, and she did not follow them herself. When the student body found out, they constantly reminded Tina that she could not tell them what to do because she was not doing what she was enforcing. Tina did not lead by example, which caused her followers to doubt her leadership abilities.

From that day on, Tina had to earn her respect back from her peers because they were not hearing anything she said. You might say, "Everybody makes mistakes," but consequences follow every mistake. Sometimes it is difficult to gain back trust and respect from the ones you lost it from. That is why it is so important to lead by example from the beginning. By knowing Tina's story, I hope you see how important it is to *demonstrate* what you enforce rather than just enforce it.

Point 2: Leaders Follow Other Leaders

Never make the mistake of thinking that leaders have no one to follow because that is not true. In many cases, if not all, real leaders follow real leaders. Have you ever heard of that saying that goes like this: "You are who you hang around?" I find that to be very true. A real leader will have more friends who are leaders than those who are not leaders. Why? Because iron sharpens iron, which means that if you want to be better, you must be around people who can make you better.

The president of the United States of America, President Barack Obama, has to lead an entire country. He makes many important decisions, and he is an extremely busy man. However, even though he is a leader, he still takes the advice of other leaders, such as his cabinet members. He is very confident that he can get the job done, but he does not let pride rise in him and cause him to reject help and advice from other leaders, such as the Vice President, Speaker of the House, Secretary of State, Secretary of Treasure, and many others. He shows that even though he is a leader and the leader of this great country, he is able to follow other leaders.

You should be the same way as President Obama. Know within yourself that you are a great leader, but do not be scared to take advice and follow other leaders, because you do not know everything. I have to remember the same thing as well. I am a leader, and I follow other leaders on a day-to-day basis.

Point 3: You Can Be a Great Leader

Do you want to make a difference in the lives around you? Do people come to you for advice? If so, you might already be a leader. Even if you are shy, you can still be a leader. The skills to become a leader can be taught, and you can learn them.

In middle school and high school, you can join clubs and organizations such as, the Debate Club, Future Business Leaders of America (FBLA), Student Council, and many others. You can watch others as they lead or take an active leadership role, such as becoming the secretary or president of a club.

In college, Phi Beta Lambda is a great leadership organization where you can gain business skills, communication skills, and many other skills that can make you a better leader. Also, it gives you many opportunities to speak in front of an audience and participate in various competitions locally and across the state. In the community, you can volunteer at various organizations, such as, Habitat for Humanity, the Boys and Girls Club, and many others. If there's not an organization in which you are interested in being a part, start your own organization or business. Many successful people became who they are today because they had an idea or saw a need and decided to start a company. You might be surprised, but some of them were young like you.

To build your leadership skills, associate with people who are leaders. Develop your speaking and communication skills through classes at your school or in the community. An excellent organization that helps you do this is Toastmasters International. Also, let your instructor (or employer) know of your desire to become a leader, and ask him or her to help you.

However, before you decide to become class president, you should know that being a leader isn't easy. Being a leader requires hard work, sacrifice, dedication, continuous learning, integrity, and much more. So, why should you lead others? What's in it for you? When you become a leader, you have the influence to change people and situations in positive ways. Also, you are responsible for moving ideas forward. In addition, leaders guide and inspire others. Last, you can make a living putting your leadership skills to use as a business.

Affirmation
"I declare that I will be a great leader because I will lead by example. I will also do my best to lead people in the right direction."

Reflect
DO YOU THINK THAT YOU ARE ABLE TO BE A LEADER?

To help you find out, start with the questions:

- ➢ Do you trust in yourself?
- ➢ Are you able to lead by example?
- ➢ Are you confident that you can lead and still follow other leaders?

Record
After you've reflected on these questions, write your thoughts here.

_____
_____
_____
_____
_____
_____
_____
_____
_____

What advice would you give someone who is having trouble being a leader who leads by example?

_____
_____
_____
_____
_____
_____
_____
_____
_____

What are some qualities of effective leaders? Name at least five. Why are they important?

_____
_____
_____
_____
_____
_____
_____
_____

Remark

What are some factors you should consider when deciding to take a leadership role?

_____
_____
_____
_____
_____
_____
_____
_____

Leaders need to be able to effectively communicate. Why is this important?

_____
_____
_____
_____
_____
_____
_____
_____

In what areas are you leading by example at school, home, work, in the community or among friends?

_____
_____
_____
_____
_____
_____
_____
_____

Respond

What steps can you take to help you become a successful leader? When will you take these steps?

ACTION   **DATE**

Rewrite the quote from the first page of this chapter in your own words.

_____
_____
_____
_____
_____
_____
_____
_____
_____
_____
_____
_____
_____
_____
_____
_____
_____
_____
_____
_____
_____
_____
_____
_____
_____
_____
_____
_____
_____

THE PARADOXICAL COMMANDMENTS
By Kent M. Keith
Printed with permission

1. People are illogical, unreasonable, and self-centered. Love them anyway.
2. If you do good, people will accuse you of selfish ulterior motives. Do good anyway.
3. If you are successful, you will win false friends and true enemies. Succeed anyway.
4. The good you do today will be forgotten tomorrow. Do good anyway.
5. Honesty and frankness make you vulnerable. Be honest and frank anyway.
6. The biggest men and women with the biggest ideas can be shot down by the smallest men and women with the smallest minds. Think big anyway.
7. People favor underdogs but follow only top dogs. Fight for a few underdogs anyway.
8. What you spend years building may be destroyed overnight. Build anyway.
9. People really need help but may attack you if you do help them. Help people anyway.
10. Give the world the best you have and you'll get kicked in the teeth. Give the world the best you have anyway.

© Copyright Kent M. Keith 1968, renewed 2001. The Paradoxical Commandments were written by Kent M. Keith as part of his book, *The Silent Revolution: Dynamic Leadership in the Student Council*, published in 1968 by Harvard Student Agencies, Cambridge, Massachusetts. More information is available at www.paradoxicalcommandments.com.

8

THE EFFECTS OF THE MEDIA

"We perceive and are affected by changes too subtle to be described."
~Henry David Thoreau (1817 – 1862)
American author, poet, and philosopher

Do you think that someone who you don't know personally can influence you to behave in a certain way? When you listen to the radio, you're being influenced in one way or another. When you watch television or look at magazine ads, you are being influenced. Influence, in this instance, means to persuade you to react to something or to think a certain way. For example, you might sing a song that contains foul language that you heard on the radio. Although you do not normally use foul language, you justify singing the song because it's not really *that* bad. Or you see a commercial on television and now you must have that new phone because the old phone (which is still usable and hi-tech) is "so last year."

What exactly is media? Media is the various means of communicating to a large group of people, such as television, radio, magazines, newspapers, billboards, and the Internet. What does this have to do with you? You are actually affected by the media more than you think. Many of your beliefs and actions are a result of what you've seen or heard, and many times you do not realize it because the messages are so subtle. Once you *agree* to the message, you *accept* it as normal, *approve* it as true, and act on it, oftentimes unknowingly.

Point 1: What You Listen to Matters

Music

Meet Kaitlyn. Kaitlyn is a sophomore in high school who said that, "It doesn't matter if a boy calls a girl the "B" word in a song because I know that he isn't talking to me." Most of the girls in that class agreed and said that it was not harmful to listen to songs where they are being called the "B" word because the song was not written to them. Some girls said that they mainly listened to the beat of the song, so the words didn't matter anyway, despite the fact that the words were very demeaning, disrespectful, and should have been embarrassing to them.

Kaitlyn thought that the words were not harmful (agreed with them) and began to accept them as just part of the song or as the way boys talked about girls. Then she approved them and acted on them by listening, singing, and dancing to the words of the song. What she didn't realize is that they words that she sang became a part of her, and she began to behave in a way that a young lady should not behave.

When songs are offensive, you can choose not to listen to them.

In addition, Kaitlyn also did not realize that when someone demeans a girl, whether it is through a song, in person, or on television, he or she demeans *all* girls, in my opinion. For instance, if a singer does not specifically mention a girl's name in a song but is referring to her by using curse words, the singer is talking about you also. Why? The reason is simply because you are a girl. Girls and women are of the same make up (even though we look differently and have different experiences) and what affects one of us should affect all of us.

Therefore, all girls, young ladies, and women should respect each other and demand that respect from the opposite sex also. It's not cool to disrespect each other or let others disrespect us. Just think: If every girl would stop listening to songs from both male and female artists that disrespect them or treat them as sex objects, we would see an increase in the self-esteem of young girls and probably a decrease in violence against them. Let's stand strong and stand together.

Point 2: What You See Matters

Television

Watching television can be an entertaining and even educational way to pass the time away, and many people block out several hours during their day to watch television. While some television programs are wholesome, others show adults, as well as teens, engaging in sexual relationships and rebellious behavior. Still, other programs glamorize women getting married several times and sleeping with different men with few, if any, consequences. However, consequences for these actions are lasting and sometimes life-changing.

Many reality TV shows that are geared to teens suggest, intentionally or not, that getting pregnant as a teenager is not such a big deal. This is far from the truth. Becoming pregnant before you are married and are able to emotionally and financially take of your child is a very serious matter and changes your life forever.

Other popular shows that follow the lives of housewives give the impression that verbally and physically fighting with other women is acceptable and normal. Programs that glamorize girls being mean towards other girls convey that it's cool to bully others and to treat them with disrespect. In actuality, these shows reveal the mean girls' serious character flaws and make her very unattractive. Remember, a girl can be very pretty to look at, but her attitude and behavior can make her very ugly.

Some female reality TV stars show us that you don't have to have morals to have money. In fact, some of them became rich because of their lack of principles. As a result, they have a terrible reputation among men. However, these same celebrities are the people who have millions of Twitter followers or television viewers who want to know what they are thinking or doing. Some girls have goals to become a reality TV star, but this life comes at a high price. The money that reality TV stars make may be tempting, but money can't buy you love, peace, or happiness. Remember, an honorable reputation and strong morals will carry you further than a big bank account, especially if it was obtained the wrong way.

What you must realize is that reality television is usually scripted and edited or directed for an intended effect to get you to watch the show. Reality television usually does not depict anyone's *real* life and definitely not their ideal life, so do not use these shows as a standard of how you should behave or who you should be. Choose what you watch carefully.

Music Videos

Videos are still very popular among some teenagers, both boys and girls. However, many of these videos send the wrong message to girls that they are to be used by guys for what they can do for them. Christina was a girl in the 10th grade that enjoyed watching music videos. When asked what she wanted to do for a living when she finished school, her answer was to be in a music video. I was surprised, but I realized that Christina was probably looking at this as a way to make quick money or to be popular. She saw absolutely nothing wrong with wearing hardly any clothes and dancing to music as other men and women danced, drank liquor, and threw money in the air around her. So, this was her career aspiration.

The sad truth is that many of these videos, produced mostly by men, portray girls as an object that is solely for male's sexual satisfaction. Many of the girls are dressed very seductively, posed in ways that are far from "lady-like," and are focused on getting or keeping a man. As a result, when young girls watch these videos and approve of them, many of them begin to dress in very tight, short, or revealing clothes, thinking that it is acceptable to behave this way. Regrettably, they oftentimes become labeled, targeted, and not taken seriously. This can lead to low self-esteem, depression, promiscuous behavior, and a life full of heartache. They have been influenced by the media and don't realize the cost.

Advertisements

Sometimes the message that is used in advertising is not exactly truthful. Some of the ads can make you feel that you are not "good enough" when in actuality, you are more than enough. If you flip through a magazine that is designed for teen girls or women, you will see that many of them feature beauty products and the latest fashion trends to make the reader feel that she should look a certain way.

Numerous commercials about exercising and dieting are frequently on television. Most models in these ads are slim and beautiful. As a result, these ads send the message that a person should be skinny and pretty to be accepted in society.

Many girls compare themselves to those models, and when they don't measure up, they sometimes engage in unhealthy or unnecessary behaviors, such as, using diet pills or eating very little or not at all to lose weight. They might also start acting out and develop low self-esteem because they do not look a certain way.

Don't buy into the lie that you have to fit into someone's idea of being pretty. The truth is that you are already pretty. What's more important than how you look is how healthy you are. You want to be your *best* you and be physically fit for your body type. So, take care of yourself by exercising, eating a nutritious diet, getting proper rest, and having the right people in your life. Remember, you are beautiful by your own standard, and you don't need to spend money making someone else rich just so you look pretty on the outside.

Images and advertisements are commonplace. Many forms of media are attempting to influence you to buy a product or think a certain way. However, you do not have to believe or respond to what you see or hear. When you see a commercial or billboard, watch a television program or a movie, read a magazine or comments on Facebook, watch videos on YouTube, or listen to songs on the radio or your iPod, you should ask yourself these questions: What is the message trying to get me to do or believe and why? Who is the source of this message, and what is in it for them?

Point 3: What You Say and Show Matters

The Internet and Social Media

The Internet, also known as the "information highway," puts information at a person's fingertip. You can easily get information that you are searching for just by typing in a few letters. You can also listen to music and view television shows, movies, and music videos 24/7. Many teenagers use social media like Facebook, Twitter, and MySpace, to communicate with each other. Young people use YouTube to make their own videos and upload them for the whole world to see.

Social media can be a fun way to connect with others, but the problem is that some girls (and people in general) use social media in the wrong way: to bully other girls, to tell their personal business to others who may use it against them, to let people know if they are in a relationship, and to post sexy pictures of themselves. This can be very dangerous.

Many girls enter chat rooms and unknowingly talk to "boys" who are oftentimes grown men. Some of these girls go to meet their online "friend" and, sadly, never return home. This has to be a horrifying experience for them and their parents.

Other girls use poor judgment and give out their personal information to someone who could eventually hurt them. There are also girls who send or receive nude or inappropriate pictures, which could not only be against the law but also posted for the whole world to see! Remember that once a picture or video is posted on the Internet, or a text is sent, you have no control over what happens to it. It is accessible worldwide and is difficult, if not impossible, to remove even when you delete it. Please use good judgment about this.

Facebook has changed the way people share information. Facebook is a great way to find people and to keep up with what's going on in their lives. However, when using Facebook, be sure that you do not post pictures of yourself that might be seen by others as distasteful. Imagine how you would feel if your mother, grandmother, youth leader at church, teacher, or someone you really respect saw your pictures. Would you need to remove some of them? Remember, what is acceptable to you might be inappropriate or embarrassing to another person. Therefore, when you take or post pictures, think about who might see them years from now and how you might feel about them later. You might view things differently than you do now when you are older.

Also, keep in mind that if you apply for a job, your potential employer might view your Facebook page to get more information about you. Would you want him or her to see you in revealing clothes or read your status? Do you use your status to intimidate, humiliate, or bully someone? Your words can come back to haunt you, and it is difficult to retract them once they have been posted. Use your status wisely and post words and pictures in a way that will not bring you shame or cause others pain.

Affirmation
"I will consider what the media is saying to me. If it is untrue or negative, I will not give it my time or attention."

Reflect
HOW DOES MUSIC AFFECT YOU?

How does music affect you? To find out, start with the questions:

- ❖ Have you heard the words to a song that you felt "talked down" to females, but you listened anyway? Why did you continue to listen?
- ❖ Do you think the words in songs affect you? How have they made you feel or behave?

Record

After you've reflected on the previous questions, write your thoughts in the space below:

_____
_____
_____
_____
_____
_____

Write a short letter to a producer of a television show that does not characterize women in a positive way. Explain to the producer how the show affects you, why it is offensive or what changes he or she could make to improve the woman's image. You can also choose to write a letter to a singer about a song.

_____
_____
_____
_____
_____

_____
_____
_____
_____
_____
_____
_____
_____
_____
_____
_____
_____
_____
_____

Remark

Image is everything. Do you have questionable pictures of you on Facebook or any other social media? "Questionable" means that your clothes are too tight, short, or revealing. What do your clothes and your poses suggest to others? If you are unsure, ask an adult who you trust. If your pictures are questionable, will you remove them?

_____
_____
_____
_____
_____
_____
_____

How can your pictures and your status on Facebook and other social media affect you?

_____
_____
_____

_____
_____
_____
_____

Optional Activities
1. Look through magazines and analyze the ads. What are they selling? Who is the product for? What images are they using to sell the products? What message do you get from the ad?
_____
_____
_____
_____

2. Pay attention to the lyrics of songs you listen to and examine the message behind the songs. Are these songs for males or females? How do you feel when you listen to them?
_____
_____
_____
_____
_____
_____
_____
_____

Respond

What steps can you take against being influenced by the media? When you will take these steps? (What date?)

ACTION   **DATE**
_____
_____
_____
_____

Rewrite the quote from the first page of this chapter in your own words.

THE INFLUENCE OF THE MEDIA

When I look in magazines, many of the ads of I see
are telling me the way I am is not how I "should" be.
There are ads with beauty products to hide my blemishes:
Make-up, bronzers, lipsticks – the list seems endless:

Diet pills and exercise bikes to help me lose weight,
5" heels with studs or spikes to wear on a date;
Teeth whitener, skin brightener, and color for my hair.
Sheer shirts and mini-skirts – wear them if I dare.

When I watch television, many women I see
are portrayed in roles subserviently:
Many of them are desperate while others curse and fight;
some are seductresses or mistresses for the night.

When I look on Facebook, some of the things I see
bring sadness and embarrassment to the woman in me:
Some people leave little to the imagination
and give personal information without hesitation.
Other girls use their status as a social apparatus
to bully and tease and do what they please.

When I listen to certain music, the words are so disgraceful.
I wonder why people buy music so distasteful:
Words that promote violence and stereotypes;
sex, drugs, profanity with drama and hype;
words that glorify violence without any shame,
and demean my worth in exchange for fame.

So, I will not listen to music or read articles in magazines,
nor watch TV programs if the message is not clean.
I will not let the media dictate how I feel,
but instead dissect the messages and decipher what is real.

Copyright 2012, Rhonda G. Mincey

RESOURCES FOR TEENS AND YOUNG ADULTS

Abuse
- Loveisrespect.org - The ultimate resource fostering healthy dating attitudes and relationships; provides a safe space for young people to access information and help in an environment that is designed specifically for them; and ensures confidentiality and trust so young people feel safe and supported—online and off. www.loveisrespect.org

Communication/Skill Building
- The Write Source - A group of teachers and writers who develop materials for students and instructors from kindergarten through twelfth grade. www.thewritesource.com

- Toastmasters International - Toastmasters International is a world leader in communication and leadership development. www.toastmasters.org

- Talk: Teen Art of Communication by Dale Carlson

Drugs
- Mind over Matter - Dedicated to teaching youth about the effects of drug abuse on the body and brain. www.teens.drugabuse.org

- Drug Abuse Resistance Education - National program designed to educate kids on the importance of avoiding drugs, gangs, and violence. www.dare.com

- Teen-Anon - For articles on drugs, alcohol, treatments and other issues visit Teen-Anon.
  www.teen-anon.com

Entrepreneurship

- Network for Teaching Entrepreneurship - Providing programs that inspire young people from low-income communities to stay in school, to recognize business opportunities and to plan for successful futures.
  www.nfte.com

- Your Teen Business. – A website with great resources by a teen entrepreneur.
  www.yourteenbusiness.com

Educational Assistance

- The College Board - Need help planning for college and preparing tools to help you succeed? Visit the College Board website and get connected with your college(s) of choice.
  www.collegeboard.com

- Fastweb Scholarships - Search for scholarships, get student financial aid and find money to pay for college.
  www.fastweb.com

- Upward Bound - Providing opportunities and support for its participants in their performances and educational pursuits.
  www2.ed.gov/programs/tiroupwardbound.com

- Junior Achievement – A nonprofit organization educating youth on business, economics, and entrepreneurship.
  www.ja.com

Job Assistance
- Career One Stop - Tools to help job seekers, students, businesses, and career professionals. Sponsored by the U.S. Department of Labor.
www.careeronestop.org

- Career Builders - The place to post resumes.
www.careerbuilders.com

- Monster - Use Monster's resources to create a resume, search for jobs, prepare for interviews, and launch your career.
www.monster.com

Leadership Organizations/Opportunities
- Do Something - Encouraging young people to make a difference in their community while providing them with the resources and support needed to do so.
www.dosomething.org

- Boys and Girls Club of America - Inspiring and enabling young people to realize their full potential as productive, responsible, and caring citizens.
www.bcga.org

- Girls Scouts of America - Helping girls to develop their full individual potential by relating to others with increasing understanding, skill, and respect.
www.girlscouts.org

- Youth Leadership - An online information center for youth leadership education and development. For teachers, parents, kids, and teens!
www.youthleadership.com

Mentoring
- National Mentoring Partnership - The #1 source for youth mentoring in the United States. www.mentoring.org

Peer Pressure
- Everything You Need To Know About Peer Pressure by Robyn M. Feller

- Teens Health - A safe, reliable resource for teens in need of professional advice or information from healthcare professionals 24 hours a day. www.kidshealth.org/teens and www.girlshealth.gov

- Above the Influence - It's about being yourself and not letting negative influence get to you. www.abovetheinfluence.com

- Boost Up - Striving to make a difference in the lives of at-risk dropouts by giving them support. www.boostup.org

Volunteer Opportunities
- Habitat for Humanity International- A nonprofit ecumenical Christian organization providing decent, affordable housing for people in need. www.habitat.org

- AmeriCorps- Assisting with the critical needs in communities all across America through partnerships and nonprofit organizations. www.americorps.gov

- American Red Cross - A volunteer-led, humanitarian organization that provides emergency assistance, disaster relief and education inside the United States. www.redcross.org

- Volunteer.org - Most reliable source of information in regards to national and local volunteer opportunities. www.volunteer.org

Youth Homelessness and Runaway Prevention
- 1-800-RUNAWAY - Keeps America's runaway, homeless, and at-risk youth safe and off the streets. 1800runaway.org

BIBLIOGRAPHY

(2010). Fascinating facts about diamonds. *GIA*.

    http://www.gia.edu/nav/toolbar/newsroom/articles-for-public/article-diamonds-fascinating-facts.html.

Kent K. (2001). The paradoxical commandments. New York: G. P. Putnam's Sons.

Notes

Notes

Notes

HELP US HELP OTHERS

The RG Mincey Group, LLC is a social enterprise. This means that we apply an entrepreneurial approach to addressing social issues and creating positive community change.

The sales of our books enable us to *"put the power of a positive, promising, and productive life"* in the hands of girls and women through life-changing books, workshops, and mentoring. In addition, the revenue that we generate allows us to make monetary donations to nonprofit organizations who directly serve these vulnerable populations. Thank you!

For more information and sponsorship opportunities, please **visit our website today at www.thergmg.com.**

STAY CONNECTED

Congratulations! You have completed *A Girl's Guide to Becoming Great*. Now put your "new mindset for life" to work by staying connected with us. Visit:

www.thergmg.com

- ❖ Download our podcasts
- ❖ Share your success stories
- ❖ Join our discussion blog
- ❖ Like, follow, and subscribe to us on social media
- ❖ Purchase books to help other groups
- ❖ Ask about bringing a workshop to your school, church, or community

We can't wait to hear from you!

ABOUT THE AUTHOR

Rhonda G. Mincey is the director of The RG Mincey Group, LLC. She is an advocate for the success, development, and well-being of young girls that come from various walks of life. She firmly believes that all young girls are beautiful, valuable, and loved, regardless of any circumstances or challenges that may confront them. Rhonda is a recipient of the Turner Broadcasting System's (TBS) prestigious *Pathfinders* Award, an award given to an individual that has positively impacted the community. She has a Bachelor's Degree in Criminal Justice and is pursuing her Master's Degree in Education. In addition, Rhonda is a poet who enjoys encouraging others through her poetry. She is married with three adult children.

CPSIA information can be obtained at www.ICGtesting.com
Printed in the USA
LVOW101432280113

317554LV00008B/69/P